BLACK LOTUS

Gratitude

Thank you to my muses along this journey for being the canvas to my mosaic. For your own unique ways of guiding me back to love.

Gratitude to my Mentor Kieona for guiding me through this beautiful metamorphosis

and supporting me through the entire journey. And for **YOU** reading who is pouring so much back into me by picking up this book and taking a step in my world.

This book is a journey of self-discovery and evolution, ego shattering, and unconditional love.

May the energy in these pages remind us there is no rush on our healing.

We are exactly where we are supposed to be.

Even in the darkest of hours the sun will soon rise again.

So will we.

Welcome to the birthplace of Phoenix Soul-Fire

Grounding

Inhale

fill up your lungs

Exhale

let your shoulders go

be still in love

Invocation

Remember...

Remember the choices we make today will
determine our tomorrow.
So let us decide to be courageous and true.
Let us follow spirit in all that we do.
Let us value love over trends.
Let us value all lives
and all bodies a love that knows no end.
Let us never stop uttering words that taste
like honey dripping down grateful lips.
Let us fall in love with ourselves every time
we walk by one another.
The greatest strength is remembering that we
are all mirrors;
the beauty, strength, and courage you witness
in me,
is a reflection of the God/Goddess in you.

Let our silence move mountains and our words
be rooted in truth.

Let our ancestors rejoice our decisions
because they are made with intention and
integrity.
Let us enjoy making love with the wind instead
of fighting against it.
Let the buzz of hummingbirds inspire us to fly
fearlessly.
Let our past be just that and lay our regrets
to rest.
Let our falls become lessons that make us
wiser
and our scars be a roadmap to our freedom.

Let us breathe in until our lungs are full of
love,
let us exhale until we have cleansed our
bodies of all the debris weighing us down.

This is your invitation to evoke the
relentless fire that dwells in you.
This is your invitation to unveil the magic
that exists because you rose this rising.

This is your invitation to come out of hiding

greet that sun that smiles contagiously at the
sight of you showing up as your best
This is your invocation
This is your reclamation of freedom
This is your time
OUR time to remember
WHO the fuck we are.

-The phoenix within

The most powerful thing is to endure a

contrasted life full of love and loss.

To withstand the winds that ferociously bellow

against us with an open heart.

The bravest thing in living such a tumultuous

life is to

write of our pain

write of our love

create gardens out of stones

breathe life into each page even when our

hands tremble

But

To share that story with the world...

To stand there naked bare in truths

with nothing clothing our deepest most

vulnerable assets

well

that my friend

is nothing less than heroic.

-The life of a poet

They say the best way to start is to just do
it.
But what if starting feels like a crater in
your chest, starting feels like reliving the
most painful of memories you've worked so hard
to forget?
What if starting means you have to face the
reality that there is a darkness that dwells
inside of you hungry and encompassing?

Then they say, "do it anyway".
Without truly understanding that there's a
difference between pushing yourself and

triggering yourself without the means to pull
yourself out of the darkness.
The ones that say "do it anyway", will they be
there when your darkness caves in on you?

When breathing feels like thorns pressing into
your spleen?

When your thoughts tangle webs around your
eyelids and all you can see is the past you've
tried for centuries to escape.
"Do it anyway".
Put yourself back into a state of hysteria.
Drown yourself in darkness.
Swallow any bit of light you've worked
tirelessly to create
"Just do it anyway",
Cause what if…
When you surrender to the darkness that is in
you
When you face the shadow and embrace it with
open arms
Confront fear with understanding
Console those parts of you that too need to be
nurtured and loved…
That you will stop reaching for support and
hold yourself

You'll realize there aren't two parts of you
but a part of you untouched

You'll drop to your knees and stop asking for
a way out and let yourself in

You'll stop praying for their pardon and ask
yourself for forgiveness for neglecting you
You'll realize that…

the darkness itself is truth simply untouched
by light
It will burst through you as love.
Because you did it anyway,
For you.

And you'll truly find peace
Make amends with the past,
And unshackle your own chains.

-Gate keeper

Woman...

My, my, my
What a gift it is
To breath in the same air as she
To experience the sway of tree branches that
move to her heart beat
My, my, my
What a gift it is
What a blessing it is to receive a gift so
supernatural
The frequency of her voice
A symphony
Orchestrated only by the most divine God
Crafted with notes of honey
Cinnamon
And ruby
Dazzling delight, it is to witness her in true
form
A 1000 petal lotus who sings to the sun
An angel cloaked in flesh and human blood
My, my, my
What a gift it is
She calms the most tumultuous of storms with
the batter of her eye lashes
She births nations of love on her exhale

She soothes pain with her compassionate ears

Allowing you to feel seen,

be heard,

and trust you are never alone

She's a poem with no words

She's a love song with no verse

She's a timeless being,

Just because she exists

So can you imagine

What healing will come to this planet

When she sees what we relish in daily?

When her third eye opens to the beast within

awaiting her awakening

What peace will come of her embracing,

evoking,

and embodying

her ability to be

The soil, the breeze, the flame, and the sea

My, my, my

What a gift it is

To breathe in the same air as she

- Elemental woman

There is no greater power than a woman with
imagination, love, and faith
She breathes fuchsia and chartreuse into a
world of black and white
She births symphonies out of screams of
respite
She blossoms chrysanthemums out of concrete
She evokes freedom out of misery
She releases pain from your heart by loving
you despite
She sees the good in all
She turns words into poetry
She lives in solitude yet makes you feel she's
always by your side
She speaks every dialect, her tongue the
language of love
She is a warrior
A Goddess
The ethers and the moon
She makes a house into a home
A boy into a King
A root into a tree
A thought into reality
She is the epitome of grace

Her laughter brings the sun out amidst the
clouds
Her smile, refreshing like lemonade on a
scorching August day
Her existence is the inspiration to love
harder, to live fully, and to forgive
She is our greatest gift
Because she loves us even when we neglect to
love ourselves
She holds us with no expectation
There is nothing she cannot do

-Wombman

Who told you?
Who told you that the size of your waist,
The color of your skin,
The fullness of your lips,
Your sexual preference,
And the twang of your accent,
Made you any more or less than the woman
sitting next to you?
Who convinced you that in order to be loved
you have to look a certain way,
That in order to be seen you have to weigh a
certain weight,
That to be beautiful means you fit within
these lines,
That a woman is merely what lays between her
thighs,
Who fed you these lies?
Who told you that femininity lays in your
physique, hair, breast, and ass makes a woman,
That it's in your best interest to swallow
your opinions and just nod your head,
Who told you these bitter lies? Who conceived
these falsifies and poured them into your milk

as a child, Told you to drink up and not waste
a drop,
Who told you that good girls do as they are
told, That good girls keep secrets of bad men
shattering their innocence,
Who told you that your worth is in your
ability to birth a child,
And that if you cannot or do not desire, well
than you are not woman at all,
Who told you that your body wasn't your
choice? Who told you that your art is not a
good investment,
Who told you that your love is on the back
burner of security,
Who told you that marriage means a church and
useless paperwork,
Who told you your dreams were mere rubbish to
be discarded in Sundays' trash bins,
Who told you that just your presence wasn't
gift enough,
Who told you!?

- 

Release...

I roll out of bed and get dressed for the day
Yet have no intentions to leave this space
No intentions to reveal myself to the world
No intentions to leave this safe container of
my apartment
Last night, I spoke to a previous partner
He revealed that he is ready when I am
His heart never released me
Says he is open to what wonders we could truly
be
To let him know when I am ready he says
And while it sounds good to my ears
My anxiety is triggered
My shoulders curl in and my body forms a ball
Why does commitment frighten me?
It ignites the flight in me and all I want to
do is hide inside of me
Wrapped up in my own body
Why does long term commitment make me forget
to breathe?
Swallow my tongue and forget how to speak
All I can do is write
Write of this plague I feel called true love

What happened to me that true untainted love
triggers me into depression
Why I rather have short term connection than a
life full of real love
Why can't I trust
that I deserve a love that divine
Why do I constantly feel like I'm stuck in
time without a way out
And life well it continues to pass me by
One heart-broken partner at a time

- *Adjustment disorder*

I have a sickness
Where I get a thought and my mind attaches
to it
it haunts me in every waking hour
it compresses my chest in my sleep
I have a difficult time with too many choices
But feel suffocated without enough options
I feel indecisive and the thought of long-term
commitment makes my whole-body ache
I love to be in love, yet I find my ways to
leave anytime someone falls in love with me
I like order yet I feel a hot mess
I love sweets and yet savory entices me
I often feel discontent with my current
situation
I developed the habit of buying things to ease
my anxiety
Just to receive it get home and realize I had
no need for it in the first damn place
I want to be loved, adored, and cared for yet
I want to be alone and in my own world

I quickly learn languages and yet I rather not
speak

I can play many instruments and yet sounds
irritate me

I feel disconnected to this body
Unsettled in this skin
Yearning for me and yet desiring the bliss of
nothingness
I have a sickness
And it spreads rapidly
I watch one by one as my once best friends
fade away because I haven't maintained our
connections
I observe as my friends start planning
weddings and talk of babies
And I can't get myself to unravel to the point
of truly wanting to unfold,
to let go
I am attached to the past yet
want nothing more than to be reborn again
I am burning from the inside out
My inner world a furnace

My outer world
frozen still
I feel trapped in my own hell

And yet all they speak of is my beauty
My light and my ability to make them feel
alive
How is this so when I feel
I have been walking dead for centuries
Drowning for eons
Encaged for decades
If only I too believed that this sickness, I
feel can be relieved
If only I was able to truly see what they see
And release the Phoenix in me
Set myself free
Release all that misery and plant seeds
Then
Then, I could blossom into the Queen I am
destined to be

- a spell

Soul ties...

Perhaps falling in love is just that
Allowing yourself to truly fall
Without the debilitating fear of who you are
when you're down there
But igniting the furious curiosity of who
you'll be when you rise again.

- Untitled

He sent me a message telling me to "get out of
his dreams",
A message that after 7 years past of us laying
entangled in sheets drenched in poetry did not
surprise me.
Though our tart and tantalizing love story has
not been one particularly missed
The sounds of his literature between my hips,
The warmth of his dialect tracing down the
nape of my neck,
The pulse of his heartbeat between my breasts
never dissipated
Only calmed.
Because even a lioness knows that in order to
feast
she must first become the grass that conceals
her
A calmness that comes with confidence.
This King I speak of knows his fate
He knows,
Even though he entertains
Radiant women
His true destiny has been with *one* all along.
He admits,

I etch my love letters in tree stumps so she
may find me on her path home.
I whisper melodies into the wings of
butterflies that land on her shoulder in
springtime.
I fuse myself into food she so tastes me in
every bite,
I have always been the first rain drop that
gently kisses her forehead in summer.
I have always been the ink in her pen when she
craves to write.
I am the pause before the exhale that soothes
her soul.
I am the arch in her back when she caresses
her body.
The nectar that drips down her thighs
The teeth mark she embeds on her lips when she
reaches the pinnacle of pleasure.
I have always been and always will be
the sun between her cheeks

The moon at her window sill that read her to
sleep

Twinkling peacefully
waiting for her
to simply remember...
Me

- Moonlight

It's nights like these I wish I hadn't told
you to back off
nights like these where every time my thighs
meet
I feel the moisture of your lips
The sweet tree sap drip
My mouth salivating
The taste of you stuck in my throat
Your smell embedded on the back of my neck
I wish I could call you back in
Open up to you
Have you show me just how much you've missed
the way you perfectly fit in
The warmth of your skin
The way my body hugs you tight
I wish I could tell you to come over
See the thing is
These fingers no longer have your number
etched on their tips
Your name no longer engraved into these lips
Your soul no longer a hold on mine
This temple is no longer your home

But it doesn't change the fact that every now
and again I feel you creep into my dreams pull
me close and grant my wish
And unravel all my resistance
I know because…
My sheets tell me so in the morning

- *Wet dreams*

The very thought of you splits me open like a
cave
A waterfall cascading down my legs
Powerful
Waking every rising
With drenched sheets
The scent of you like initials carved on my
tree trunk like heart
The air tastes like you
The ocean holds onto our truths
Of you and I kissing in rainstorms
and creating rainbows with our tongues
Us making love on the balcony of fate
whilst the whole world watch
And embrace
You make music with my body
And it will never make sense
How we make such art 1000s of miles away

- Borderless love

Black Lotus
Love does not hurt
Love is soft like sea moss underneath your
toes
Textured and dense
Why do we become hopeless in the name of love?
Because we seek romance and *call it love*
A tree is not a flower
A wasp is not a honeybee
Romance is not love
Do not give up on love
Love never did anything but embrace you
unconditionally

- A love poem

You reached for my hand and said "just kiss
me",
I blushed and never reached back
And while the desire is there
While I enjoy the soft stumble of your chin
hair caress my cheek
while we dance under moon lit nights under the
banyan tree
While swaying sweetly to the scent of the
ocean breeze
While sand beneath our feet as we walk along
the beach
While learning about what wine goes best with
salad
And practicing how to do everything with
passion
While we discuss our ideology of love
And build trust
Laying under my blush pink canopy
Listening to the soothing tunes of vinyl
gazing into the blue lagoons of your eyes

I cannot kiss you

I cannot bear witness to yet another beautiful
flower being wilted by my selfishness
Another incredible man falling into me
endlessly and watching him fall
while I haven't the capacity to catch him

I cannot accept your heart in my hand
To kiss you would be to welcome you in
Because it starts with the kiss of your soft
lips
That write love songs along mine
And the tongue that writes love letters on
mine
And the fingers that dance tango inside of me
That leads to the same story

Me loving you when it's convenient for me
And wasting time that you could be investing
in someone who will allow themselves to fall
into you without fear
With the capacity to see every misalignment as
an opportunity to grow and expand in love

The woman that you deserve

I don't want you to miss her because you are
engulfed in me

- The first kiss

I was so certain about what our love was
And that it best from afar
That with time we'd move on
That he was flourishing in love with another
And that he was better off without me
And then he wrote me
"Hi, we miss you. We love you. We think of you
often."
And when I told him, "I was calling to you in
my dreams…" and asked him…
"Have you heard me?"
He said
"call me plz"
And so I did
Without hesitation
I listened to my spirit
And when his voice reached my ears
I surrendered
"Hi"
Is all he had to say
"Hi"

a chill swept my body

The pace of my heart slowed down
And the voice in my throat simmered
"Hi"
That simple word
That reminded me why I felt I had to separate
myself with such distance so that we may move
forward
In reality
I had to separate myself from my guilt
Of not loving him the way he deserved
"Hi"
The single word that melts my flesh into pools
of rose petals
"Hi"
Made me realize his love was never wavering or
lost
"Hi"
The utterance of those words
From those lips
That made my defenses shift
"Hi"
Wraps me in warm embrace
Holds me accountable
Makes love to my senses

Lays with me in every dialect
It both guards
And holds my heart

This time my
"Hi"
Greeted him with a smile
With an open heart
With no attachment to the past
No resentment for what had not been
And as my spirit revealed to me
I gave myself the fair opportunity
And so, I
Paused
And breathed him in across the ocean
Lay down my weapon and centered in my heart
This time
the version of me he had yet to meet
bowed to his beauty
The me that is familiar
Yet unknown

"Hi"
I exhaled
It's nice to finally see you,
King

- a single word

What is it like to be in love with a Phoenix?
To be willing to go to the end of the world
for her
To give the pulse of your heart to her beat
To give the breath in your chest for her to
never weep
To constantly confront your shadow, ego,
pride,
and put them aside
to uplift her
So, she may rest peacefully
To rescue her from her demons
To forgive her when she split you in two
And leave you to pick up the pieces
To find faith in her spirit when her words do
not align with her actions time after time
To bleed your heart for her every waking
moment
To journey to the other side of the world for
her
To reveal your love
And never have her love you the same
It burns
And yet

It never fades
She is embedded in your soul
And you would do it all over again

- Ex partner

They say the way to become anything is just to
start, no attachments to the past or future
just begin now.
That practice makes progress not perfection

———-

We were supposed to get married
You and me
Supposed to have beautiful brown skin babies
With dimples and Afro puffs running around
On land we've cultivated
Somewhere yonder
In the mountains
Supposed to heal the world through art
Uplift our brothers and sisters by being an
example of unconditional love
And then,
one night you called me
A night that still dwindles a knot in my belly
A night where I realized you had become
Tired
Tired of waiting for me to finally look up and
see what God has gifted to me
Tired of being forgiving in a space where
there was no shade to rest

from the blazing sun that is my demanding
personality
Tired of giving me the world when I struggled
to give myself grace
Tired of me clinging to old versions of me
that held me hostage in misery
Tired of sending love letters in bottles
across oceans while I lay sleep on the shore
Tired of hoping that one day I would open my
almond curved eyes and feel you
Hold you up with both arms and a beating heart
that pulsed for you
Just for you
Tired

And so, when you called that night
I lost my breath for a moment
I realized that your tiredness gave you no
other choice but to release me
And move forward in love
When you called and said
"P, I got someone pregnant"
I realized
That my time had run out
Yet,

The pain of losing you gave loving me a
fighting chance
the very catalyst to finally lay my ego to
rest
And practice
Reciprocity
Practice compassion
Practice embracing what's in front of me
Practice listening to learn
Practice giving not only to receive but for
mere love
Practice to make progress
Not perfection
The absence of you was the reason I finally
chose
To unshackle my own chains
And really
Practice

- Practice

The greatest love I've known is that of a past
lover and lifetime friend
They know the deepest darkest parts of you
Offer safe refuge
Have kissed your soul
Have kept secrets no one knows
Watch you fall asleep
They embody your senses
Your eyes
Ears
Your Sanity
And they never judge the inconsistencies
They hold you to your highest selves
They respect, honor, and hear your boundaries
They stay in your heart
Even when you move on
And they have to watch from a far
A new love tuck you in at night
And new umbrella to shower you from the rain

Their love is timeless
Even when the sky falls
Their love remains

- Greatest love

Purge...

Craters for shoulders

Knots in my back

Cold sweats sweep my body

No energy

To think hurts

as someone is standing on my forehead

Goosebumps breakout across my skin

Warm

Cool

Sleep

Eat

All I can do

Is surrender

When I try to fight it worsens

It is hard for me to surrender

A purge

Of all the toxins built up in my muscle's

membrane

death inside of me

And I continue to keep reaching for her hand

I am having a hard time letting her burn

Because the darkness is a part of me

I weep for her

She truly means no harm
A mere wounded child who birthed a fortress in
her out of fear
Of me trying to seize her body
Capture her innocence and enslave her spirit
She is still in there
The 6-year-old girl
Who wanted to play house just for pretend
Play with dolls and teacups
She didn't agree to be trapped in the walls of
her father's house
When her step brother said, "you be the mom
I'll be the dad"
She didn't invite being torn to pieces
When he told their younger sister, "not to
look because that's how you play"
She didn't know she was deserting me
When he slid his clammy fingers in my panties
with dirt encrusted nail beds
When he said this is what mothers and fathers
do
That perhaps they do
But not step brother and sister

That she agreed to play pretend
Instead

She attended her own funeral that day

As she lay there afraid to speak
Her soul screamed
She left her body
And abandoned that little girl
There in that bed
When her brothers came in from playing
outside, she concealed her pain
And swallowed her voice
When her father asked what was wrong
She lied
And it was then
She buried that little girl still alive
Left her there to die
So now at 31 she cries for me
To rescue her
And release her from this hell
To forgive myself and let go of the anger and
make peace
It is hard to surrender

When at such a young age all was stripped from
me
All she wants is to console me, but my fire
won't let her inside these walls

A purge reveals this darkness
Attempts to release and reset
Yet

I hold on
To what feels like safety
My hardness
My fortress
I am burning myself down while trying to
protect this old castle
I am having a hard time
Choosing love

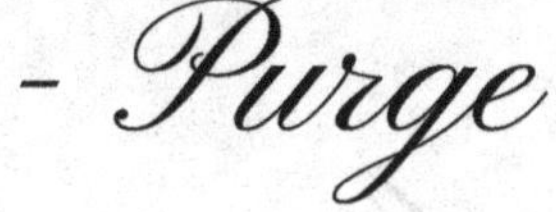

May be just maybe
One day
She will realize
That loving you does not have to mean
The need to give up her freedom
In fact,
It means the beginning of her life
A life of unconditional love
A love that will make her the most
powerful version of herself
But she must first allow herself
The gift
Of love

- Maybe

Opening...

I find it easy to write poems about my own
demise
Because I know it so well
I find it easier to create art out of blacks
and grey
Then pinks and white
I find it natural to
Sing songs about heartbreak
I find it comforting to go inwards than to
break through
And yet,
That all changed the moment I allowed myself
to fall into you

- Spring

There is no rush on love
For love takes the willingness to unfold
Love takes courage to be soft and strong
Love takes guts
Love takes the road less traveled
Love takes it's sweet time to unwind any fear
and reveal truth
Love takes patience
Love takes faith in what you cannot see with
your eyes
But feel in your spirit
Loves takes appreciation for the silence
Love takes awareness of the words unsaid
Love takes pleasure in presence
Love takes compassion
Love takes any doubt and turns it into
opportunity
For exploration

Love takes the ability to let shit go

Love takes accountability

Love takes the clouds and turns them into
shade

Love takes the sun's blaze and turns it into
warmth

Love takes the rain and turns it into double
rainbows
Love takes trust
Love takes admiration
Love takes acceptance for what is
Love takes kindness
Love takes finding the beauty in imperfections
Love takes understanding that we are the same
Love takes noticing
Love takes it's time

- a love song

I wanna know what it's like,
To allow my knees to buckle when my heart is
overjoyed in love.
I wanna know what it's like to
trust my spirit and not put up a fight.
I wanna know what it's like
to melt into you
While you swim inside my intellect.
I wanna know what it's like
to lead with my heart and not my mind.
I wanna know what it's like
to open up to you
Like endless oceans
Waves crashing against my crest

I wanna know what it's like,
To live in love
To walk in trust

To breathe in now

And exhale lust.

I wanna know what it's like

to be tied up in your manhood

peel open your layers

feel your femininity.

I wanna know who dwells inside,

The one who wraps me in his essence when I

fall asleep in your eyes.

I wanna know what it's like,

To not have to control it all,

allow you to lead,

to experience the bliss of untainted love.

I wanna know what it's like,

To release my guard

And know my walls can come crumbling down.

I wanna know what it's like,

To share the crown,

To dance in grace in ballrooms of fate.

I wanna know,

Royalty.

What it's like

to rule a kingdom beside you.

What it's like
to wash your feet
After the voyage you seek.
I wanna know what it's like
to truly Walk like the Goddess I am,
Unmask this facade of a shallow hearted woman
who clenches my heart tight.
I wanna know what it's like
to truly love me.
Because in loving me
Without conditions,
I can finally know
what it's like
to build pyramids
Love without defeat,
While we lay wake and while we sleep
I wanna know what love untamed is truly like.

- *Show me*

Dear beloved,

I know you are suffering

And I am here for you.

You do not have to suffer alone.

Allow me to hold you in sacred space.

Allow me to listen with compassionate ears.

Allow me to embrace you with love.

Allow me to sit with you through the pain.

Allow me to breathe in and out with you so we
may exhale the troubles that cause you
disdain.

Allow me to be your community.

Allow me to be an open hall where you can let
go of any past trauma that haunts you.

You do not have to weather the storm of the
world on your own.

Allow me to be your center,

Your cloak.

Allow me to uplift you when you feel heavy
with despair.

Allow me to be your temple.

Let us meditate and create a place of peace
within.

Let us confront our fears together.

Release our souls.
Let us build love in empathy.

Dear beloved,
I know you are suffering
And I am here for you.
You do not have to suffer alone.
Allow me to hold you in sacred space.
Allow me to receive some of the pain you feel,
sit beside you while we transform it into
peace.
Allow me to offer tranquility by embodying
grace.
Allow me to synchronize our breath,
So we may return back to the present.
Allow me to be the tree that stands strong in
the garden,
Unwavering and resilient.
Allow me to be the stone you sit on.
Allow me to alleviate some of your pain.

Dear beloved,
Let us build a fortress of love,
The storm will do what storms are meant to do,

The rain will undoubtedly come,

But together we can receive the gift of life.
Accept and embrace the turbulence together
So we may be able to enjoy the ride.

— *Sangha*

Rebirth...

I've been to the depths of my own demise
I've had to go to war with my ego
I've been reliant on others to save me
To pull me out
To release me from the inner hell that I created
But this time
Is different
I used my own magic to free myself
Usually, I submerge from my purge with hardness
But this time,
I've made an alliance with my softness
So she may not be cast aside when the storm comes
But be the storm
Unshakable

— Storm/Changes

What does one write about when there's no
heartache
When there's no lover to sweep you off your
feet
When there's no misery
No deceit
No torture
No self-inflicted pain
No loss
No gain

What does one write about
When there's no drama
No sad ending
No heart wrenching news
What does one write about when there's no
Prince Charming
And their forced to save themselves

We write about faith
Gratitude
And love
Because without it we lose ourselves in the
ever-changing current of life

— *Anchor*

You can't force poetry
But you can tell your story
You can write your truth
I believe we have parallels in this lifetime
And there are people who have gone through the
same strife
Believe we have soulmates we may never find
Believe we have past lives
Future selves
Reflections in both humans and nature
So, when we write
it is so we may reach the souls
Whom for so long thought
there was no one on earth who may understand
them
That in fact, there is someone out there who
shares the same story
And we are not alone

– Reflection

As I near the end of this chapter I am filled
with such joy
Recognizing that this is only just the
beginning
This journey is something I gifted myself
A sacred sanctuary where my thoughts transpire
into words that flutter across paper
My ink bleeds the sorrow of my heart and
transforms it into art
The gift is that there may be one person
reading this who is inspired to speak their
truth
An example of channeling trauma into triumph
That at the minimum I set myself free in this
journey
In this book,
I lay my restless spirit to rest
On these pages that you hold in the palms of
your hands
freedom reigns in between each line of this
piece
I began a wounded girl
Trapped in her own fallacy

And I have allowed myself the gift of
metamorphosis
Burrowed in the cocoon of my mind
melted into a pupa of feelings, emotions,
sensations
And sat in silence
Through the blistering storm
Danced with my inner child
Gone to war with my ego
And opened the door of my mind's eye
Paved a way for the Queen within me
Busted out the casing that embrace me tight
Stretched out my wings
And returned
To myself
"A Mourning Cloak Butterfly"

- Evolution

When you go through transformation
You burn away old versions of you
you rise out of the ashes
You sprout wings from your backside
And you are no longer recognizable
Because you have evolved
The people you knew before
you no longer resonate with
The things that used to be of interest are no
longer relevant
Let me tell you, it is perfectly fine
A bird isn't given wings to just stay still
and perch
Spread your wings
Even if for a moment it seems a lonely ride
Release what is not love
Not light
Not in alignment
And Fly

— *Wings*

I see now that there is no good that comes in
holding on
No good that comes with being bitter for the
things you cannot change
No use in causing unnecessary suffering by
wishing things would stay the same
It is in our highest interest to welcome the
ebb and flow
To notice when life is pulling us in a
different way
And to surrender
The most difficult but rewarding gift I have
learned
Is to let go

- Life's Lesson

I've never had a love quite like this
One that kisses and stains my lips
One that holds me in my Dreams
One that loves me in, out, and in between
I've never had a love quite like this
It lives underneath my nail beds
Coils around my hair follicles
Smeared into skin
Dancing in between my ribs
Plays love songs behind my eyelids
Wakes me up like morning tea
Hydrogen and oxygen in chemistry
Puts me to sleep like chamomile
Soothes my soul like lavender
Ignites my fire with passion
Heals my heart with transparency
I've never loved a love quite like this
It's hypnotic by nature
melodic like pleasure
Dresses my wounds with honey

Sticks to my Aura and imprints on my heart
I've never known a love so peaceful,
I am so grateful that I found me

- Reunion

Dear Me,
I am so proud of you.
You've come a long way
From looking at life as what happened
To you
to opening your eyes and giving thanks for
vision
You've been reborn again with the chance to
see the vibrancy of the world in a new light
An opportunity to plant seeds
To manifest love into every step you take
To find gratitude in every breath

Dear me,
You are no longer who you used to be
You have decided to live life fully
There will be bumps along the journey
There will be times where you feel you
misstep
Times where you feel the old you tiptoeing
around your door
Waiting for you to crumble because the growing
feels hard

Times where your ego will beg you to submit

But stand tall
Stand in your pact with your heart
join forces with freedom
Stand wise in your intuition it will guide you
through the times where your eyes cannot see
two feet in front of you.
Stand true
In your authenticity
There will be many people along the journey
who have unsettled spirits and will try to rob
you of your light
Shine brighter
Stay vigilant
And trust yourself

Dear me,
You may have to travel some places by yourself
But you are never alone
You are protected by spirits and guarded by
ancestors
The wind stands behind you
The ocean beneath you

The sun inspired by you
The moon a reflection of you

Dear me,
It is a great responsibility to possess so
much power and use it for the greater good
There will be times you grow tired
Times you wish it were anyone else but you
But god gifted you with this second chance
So that you may heal the world
Keep on shining

- Love Letter

Closing...

May this book be a catalyst to reconcile the
past, release fear, and break free so you may
live in love. That through reading this book
you feel held and supported to evoke the
divinity in you.
Mahalo,

Phoenix Soul-Fire

Stay updated on the author via social media.
Facebook: Phoenix Soul-Fire
Instagram: @phoenixsoul.fire
Website: phoenixsoulfire.com